My Senses
HEARING

by
Grace Jones

Words written in **yellow** are explained in the glossary on page 24.

CONTENTS

©2016
Book Life
King's Lynn
Norfolk PE30 4LS

ISBN: 978-1-910512-70-8

Written by:
Grace Jones
Edited by:
Gemma McMullen
Designed by:
Drue Rintoul

A catalogue record for this book
is available from the British Library.

WHAT ARE MY SENSES?

We all have 5 **senses**. They are sight, smell, taste, touch and hearing.

Your senses tell you what is going on around you.

HOW DO I HEAR?

EARS

You use your ears to hear the sounds around you.

Sound waves move through the air and into your ears.

SOUND WAVES

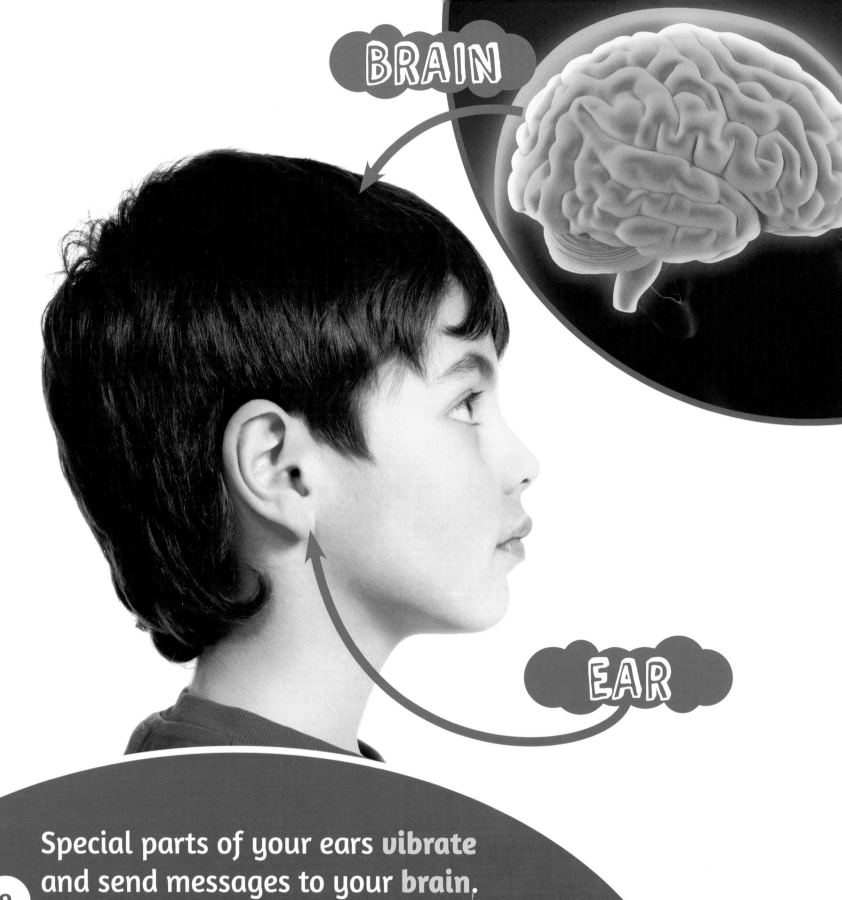

BRAIN

EAR

Special parts of your ears **vibrate** and send messages to your **brain.**

8

Your brain tells you what sounds you are hearing.

SOUNDS

VIOLIN

There are many different types of sounds in the world.

Sounds can be quie or loud, low, or high.

LOUD AND QUIET SOUNDS

When you whisper you make a quiet sound.

Fireworks make a very loud sound.

HIGH AND LOW SOUNDS

TRIANGLE

Some instruments, like the triangle, make very high sounds.

14

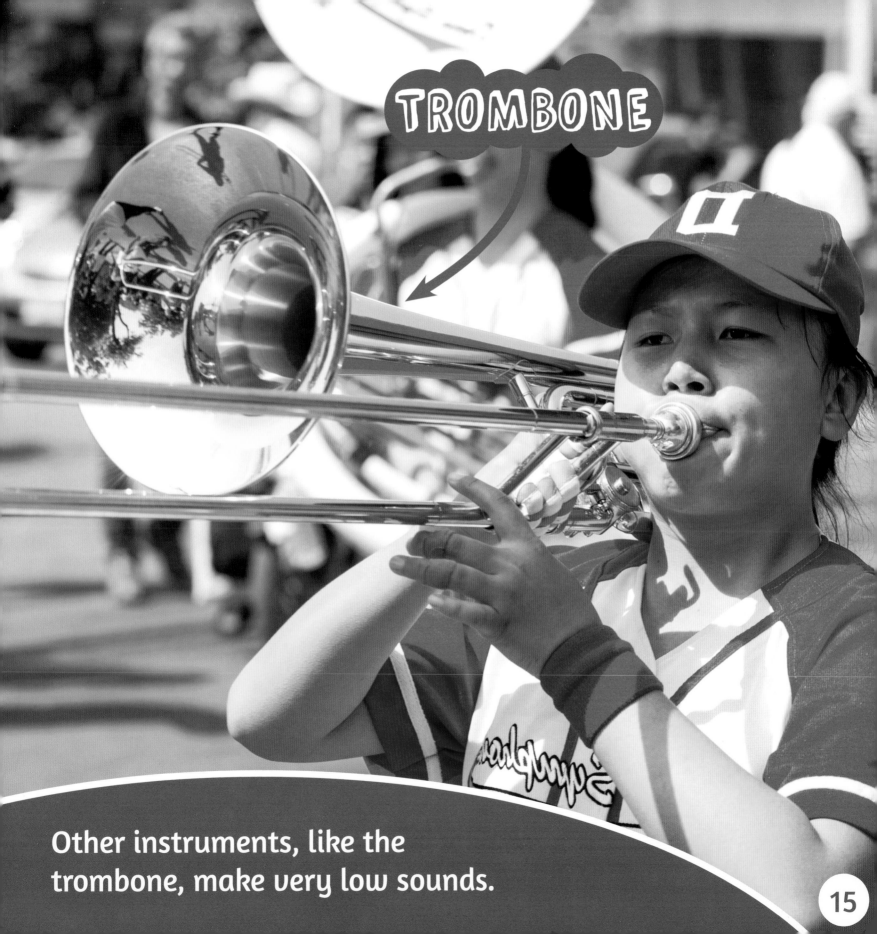

Other instruments, like the trombone, make very low sounds.

Cows make loud and low sounds.

Mice make quiet and high sounds.

STAYING SAFE

Your sense of hearing helps to keep you safe from danger.

When you hear a car coming you move out of its way.

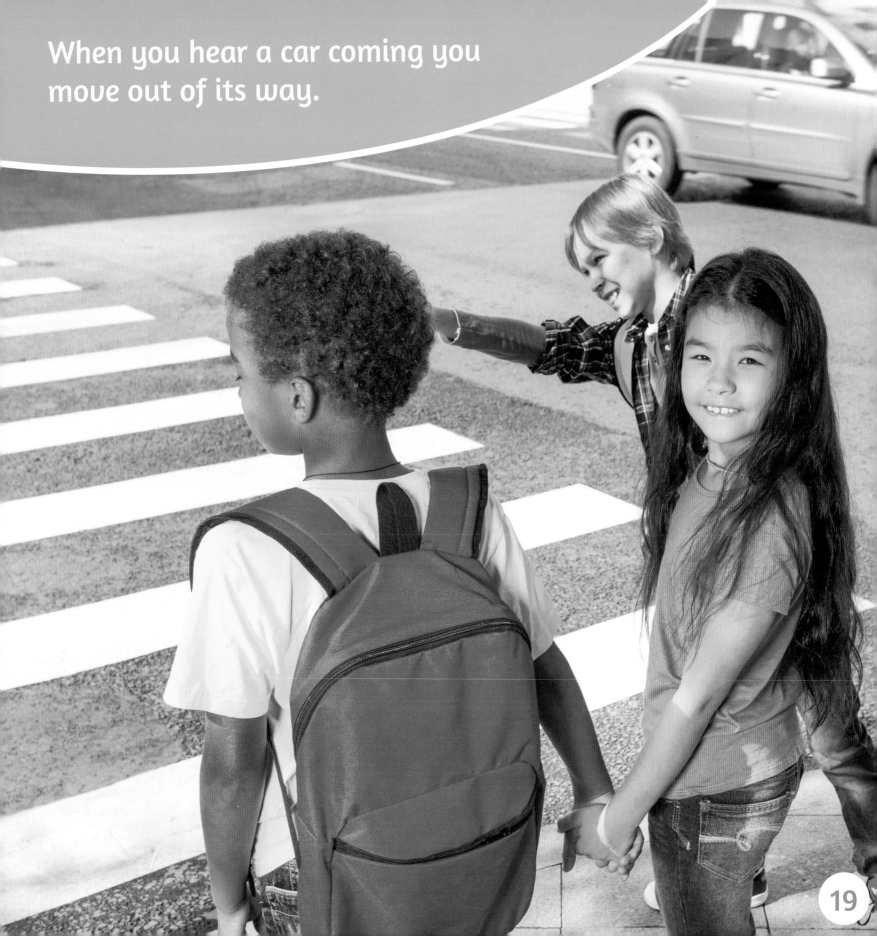

SUPER SENSES!

People who are **blind** use their hearing to help them cross the road.

They listen for loud beeps to tell them when it is safe to cross the road.

WHAT CAN YOU HEAR?

Visit your local park or garden
and close your eyes. What can you hear?

Can you tell what is making the sounds you can hear?

GLOSSARY

BLIND
someone who cannot see.

BRAIN
tells your body what to do.

SENSES
tell you what is going on around you.

SOUND WAVES
a wave made by sound that moves through the air

VIBRATE
to move side to side quickly

INDEX